My animal book

My animal book

What kind
of animal
are you?

Thames & Hudson

Let's find out....

How to use this book

Are you ready to go on an animal adventure? Animals live in all kinds of places. Some live high up in the air, some live under the ground and some live in water.

Say hello to Koko and Alex

Hi, I'm Koko. I want to find out about animals. Do you?

Which kind of animal is your favourite?

Hi, I'm Alex. Come on, let's see what we can learn.

When you see ...

... ask a grown-up to help you.

... get ready to do things.

Meet the explorers

The three explorers love animals and adventures. Join them to find out about different animals.

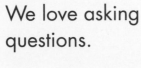
We love asking questions.

Who made these footprints?

Remember there are answers on pages 62 and 63!

OK! Let's go ...

What is an animal?

The explorers are talking about what makes an animal.

1

Is this stone an animal?

Don't be silly. Animals have legs. Stones don't have legs.

It's not only legs that make an animal. An animal is a living thing. A stone isn't.

2

What about a flower? A flower is a living thing.

Yes, but a flower is a plant, not an animal.

Plants can't move, but animals can. Look at that mouse running!

3

But a snake hasn't got legs. Is it still an animal?

Yes. Animals move in lots of different ways. Snakes slither and fish swim. Spiders walk on eight legs and birds fly.

Animal families

Which animals belong in which group?

Each kind of animal belongs to an animal group.
There are six main groups.

mammals

A mammal has fur or hair to keep warm.

Dogs, cats, monkeys and people are mammals.

reptiles

A reptile has scaly skin for protection.

Snakes and lizards are reptiles. They lay eggs.

fish

A fish has gills to breathe underwater.

Fish live underwater. They have fins to swim.

insects

An insect has six legs. Its body has three parts.

Ladybirds, grasshoppers and beetles are insects.

amphibians

An amphibian can live on water or land.

Frogs are amphibians. They lay eggs in the water.

birds

A bird has a beak and feathery wings.

Hawks and parrots are birds. Most birds can fly.

Please help me to sort out which animal belongs in which group.

To which animal group do you belong?

10

I'm a frog. I swim underwater and also jump about on land.

I'm a beetle. I scuttle on my six legs.

I swim in the sea.

I'm a hawk. I fly high up in the sky with the help of the feathers on my wings.

I'm a gorilla. Quick! My baby is hungry and needs milk.

I'm an iguana. I sit in the sun to keep warm.

Yes, that's right, you're a mammal.

Play the animal group game
Spot an animal from each animal group to win!

How to play   A game for two or more players

1. Place your counters on START.
2. Take turns to throw the die. Move along the board.
3. When you land on an animal, tick it off your list.
4. When you land on a mixed-up animal, miss a go.
5. The first player to spot an animal from each animal group is the winner.
   If you get stuck use the colours to help!

Flap your wings to fly to the next bird!

I'm mixed-up! I don't belong in any animal group. Miss a go.

Watch out! Deep water!

purple — bird
I flap my wings and peck with my beak.

blue — amphibian
I can live in water or on land.

pink — reptile
I have scaly skin.

light blue — fish
I swim using my fins. I breathe underwater with my gills.

yellow — insect
I have six legs for running and crawling.

green — mammal
I have fur or hair on my body.

12

You will need

a pencil, counters and a die

Draw six boxes on a piece of paper. Label each box with one of the animal group names, as shown.

bird	insect
I	IIII
fish	amphibian
IIII	II
mammal	reptile
III	IIII

Leap to the next amphibian!

If you haven't spotted an animal from each group, go back to the start.

Legs, tails and wings
Create a collection of stand-up paper animals!

You will need

a sheet of A4 paper

scissors

colouring pencils

Choose one of these animals or draw your own with help from a grown-up.

1

Fold the paper in half.

2

Draw and colour your animal over the fold.

3

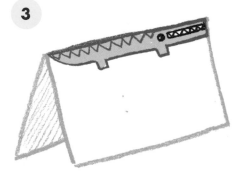

Make sure you draw the animal on both sides of the fold. It also needs legs to stand on.

4

Cut around the outline of your animal. Stand up your animal.

Your animal kingdom collection standing tall.

Make an animal flip book

What a mix-up! Flip the pages to make new animals.

You will need

4 pieces of A4 paper (1 coloured and 3 white)

pencils

stapler

scissors

Adult help needed!

1 Fold all the pieces of paper in half to make a book with the coloured paper as the cover.

2 Ask an adult to help you staple the book together at the fold.

3 Draw a different animal on each page. Draw the head at the top, the body in the middle and the legs at the bottom.

4 Cut the pages with your drawings into three parts. The head, body and legs will be on different flaps.

5 Flip the pages to make crazy animal combinations.

Hello, I'm a cat-monkey-duck!

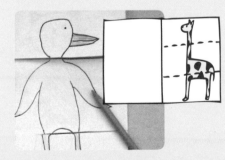

I'm a shark-bear-frog!

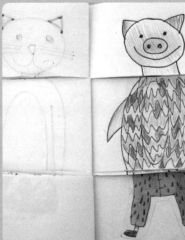

Play animal detective!

Are you ready to follow the animal footprints?

Follow the different footprints, or tracks, to find out which hungry animal has taken food from the explorers' picnic!

On the move

How does each animal move?

Fly! I use my feet to help me to land.

Slither! My claws help me to pull myself along the river bank.

Scurry! My claws help me to climb trees to find acorns.

Run, run, run! My big toes help me to run fast in the sand.

Hop! My big back feet give me extra spring.

Where do animals live?

Animals live everywhere!

They live in rainforests, high up in the mountains, in oceans and deserts. They even live in the hottest, driest and coldest places on the planet.

cold
warm
hot
warm
cold

seal

polar bear

I swim in icy polar seas.

black bear

fox

I'm happiest in the desert.

ostrich

camel

desert

Meet the world's biggest animal! Blue whales live in the ocean.

rainforest

I live in the world's largest river, the Amazon.

caiman

gorill

snake

blue whale

ocean

penguin

Arctic

Bears usually live in forests.

forest

brown bear

reindeer

I live in cold mountain forests.

eagle

The African grasslands are my home.

giant panda

elephant

grasslands

kangaroo

The kangaroo lives only in Australia.

Antarctica

19

Spot me!

What kind of animal am I? Where do I live?

How do animals survive?

Animals can live in all kinds of places, from high on a mountain to deep under the ocean.

A goat can climb to the top of a mountain.

Up in the mountains

A goat has hooves that grip the rocks tightly. It has long, thick fur to keep it warm.

Freezing cold

A polar bear has thick fur and a layer of fat to keep it warm. In the winter, a mother bear digs a den in the snow where she gives birth to her cubs.

Hot, hot, hot

In the heat of the desert, insects run fast so they don't get hot.

Can you find a camel? It stores fat in a hump on its back.

Up in the air

Birds have feathery wings to fly high up in the sky.

On land

A giraffe has a long neck to reach the leaves on tall trees.

Ponds

A frog can live in water or on land.

A frog can hop back into the water if it gets too hot!

In the ocean

Many sea creatures have a tail and fins to help them swim.

Little fish swim together in a shoal. Big fish will not eat them if they look like one big animal.

Amazon rainforest

Let's explore among the trees.

We're in the rainforest. Monkeys swing high up among the leaves, snakes crawl along tree branches, insects march across the forest floor and a caiman swims in the river.

Parrots are brightly coloured and squawk as they fly.

Canopy
Parrots fly high in the treetops.

Understorey
Animals live in the tangled branches.

An anteater has a long snout for eating ants.

Forest floor
Snakes slither along the ground.

A caiman waits in the river for lunch to swim by.

Amazon river
Piranha fish swim in the water.

A sleepy sloth hangs from tree branches most of the time.

Millions of different types of insect live in the Amazon rainforest.

One drop of poison from a poison dart frog can be deadly!

Play the spot-the-animal game.

A game for two or more players

How to play

1 Choose an animal shape. Say its name out loud.

2 Ask a friend to choose an animal and say its name too.

3 Turn the page. The first to find their animal and say its name is the winner!

1 golden lion tamarin

4 paradise phantom butterfly

2 giant anteater

3 quetzal

6 pygmy marmoset

5 poison dart frog

8 kinkajou

9 iguana

7 tapir

10 anaconda

12 capybara

11 harpy eagle

14 katydid

15 tent-making bat

16 blue morpho butterfly

17 jaguar

13 sloth

18 turtle

19 leafcutter ants

20 black caiman

24 toucan

22 spider monkey

23 peccary

21 saki monkey

28 ocelot

27 woodnymph hummingbird

25 hyacinth macaw

26 capuchin monkey

29 tree boa

30 yapok

31 pink river dolphin

23

Amazon rainforest animals

Quick! Find and name your animal.

A spider monkey has long arms and lives high up in the trees.

A capybara is like a huge guinea pig.

An anaconda squeezes its dinner to death.

Poison dart frogs are brightly coloured.

24

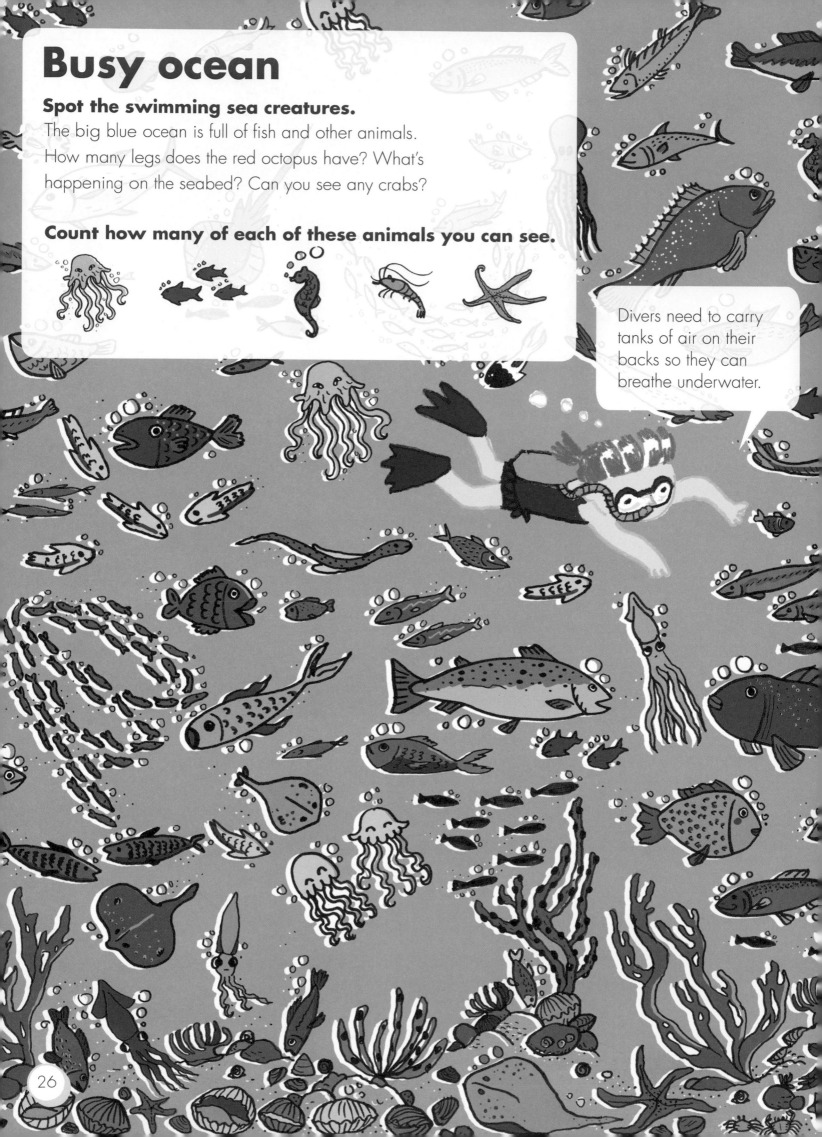

Busy ocean

Spot the swimming sea creatures.

The big blue ocean is full of fish and other animals. How many legs does the red octopus have? What's happening on the seabed? Can you see any crabs?

Count how many of each of these animals you can see.

Divers need to carry tanks of air on their backs so they can breathe underwater.

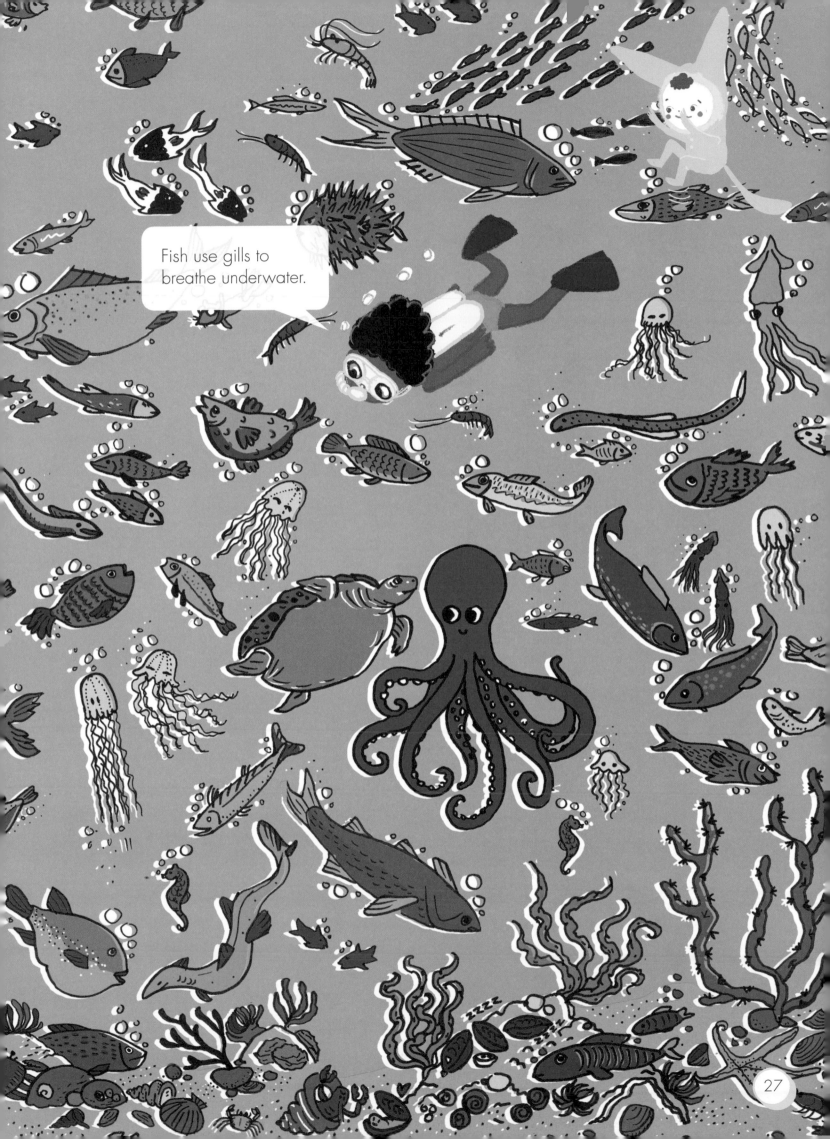

Fish use gills to breathe underwater.

Home, sweet home

1 Little Bird, Hedgehog, Squirrel and Rabbit played all day, and Squirrel invited everyone back to his house.

But Squirrel's home is in a tree! Hedgehog and Rabbit can't jump high enough to join him.

Why do you live so high up?

So I can stay safe and keep my acorns dry.

My house is underground. Let's go there!

2 Squirrel likes Rabbit's house, but Little Bird gets mud on his wings and Hedgehog's prickles get stuck!

Why don't you have a bigger burrow?

3 So nothing bigger than me like a fox can get in! It's cosy and warm.

Hedgehog suggests they go to his house.

28

4

5

6 The friends lie on Hedgehog's leaves in the sunshine.
They enjoy being together, but when they feel sleepy …

What do animals eat?

How do different animals catch their food?

When you're hungry, what do you do?
Animals have lots of ways of catching their dinner.

krill

Hair-comb mouth

The blue whale eats krill,
which are tiny shrimp-like animals.
They are so small that the whale
has a special kind of mouth
shaped like a comb to trap them.

blue whale

krill

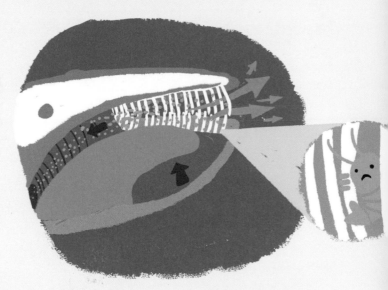

1 The whale fills its huge mouth with water and millions of krill.

2 The whale's comb-like plates trap the krill and the whale swallows them.

Super ears

To help find out where a delicious
fly is hiding, a bat makes special
sounds, then waits for the sound
to bounce back from the fly.

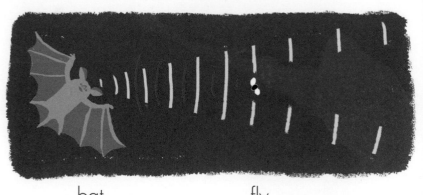

bat   fly

Clever traps

A spider catches its dinner in a trap, called a web.

1 The spider starts to build its web.

2 The spider weaves threads one way.

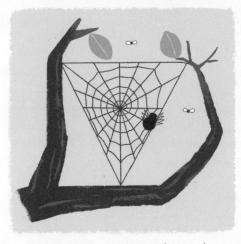

3 Then it weaves threads the other way.

4 The spider sits in the middle and waits.

5 An insect gets caught! The spider wraps up the insect to eat later.

Poison

This snake has teeth that inject poison, called venom, into the mouse.

Changing colour

The Arctic fox can sneak up on any animal it wants to eat without being seen. In summer, it has brown fur, the same colour as the ground. In winter, when it snows, the fox's fur turns white.

Brown in the summer

White in the winter

31

Play mealtime stories

Animals sometimes eat each other!

Make up funny animal stories with this 'food chain' game. When you match up the colours of the boxes, you've made a true food story.

How to play

A game for two or more players

Take it in turns to roll the die. Roll the die four times to create your story.

 Throw the die! If you roll a 1, your story starts with 'Koko …'.

 Throw again! If you roll a 3, your story reads 'Koko licks …'.

1 Koko

2 A snake

3 An elephant

4 A mosquito

5 An owl

6 A frog

1 gobbles

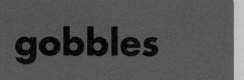

2 eats

3 licks

4 chews

5 bites

6 swallows

You will need

a die
pen and paper

A frog …
bites …
a zebra …
on the beach!
Haha!

Koko …
licks …
a spider …
under a full moon!
Ewww!

 Throw again! If you roll a 6, 'Koko licks an ice cream …'.

 Once more! If you roll a 4, 'Koko licks an ice cream on the beach.'

1  a zebra

1 in a cave.

2  a spider

2 on a bush.

3 a mouse

3 under the hot sun.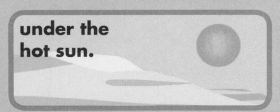

4  a worm

4 on the beach.

5 leaves

5 in a pond.

6  an ice cream

6 under a full moon.

Make animal pancakes

You will need

1 egg
250 ml milk
250 g self-raising flour
25 g butter
berries, sliced fruit, jam
and chocolate sauce
for decoration

1 Crack the egg into a large mixing bowl.

2 Add the milk.

3 Sieve the flour into the bowl with the milk and egg.

4 Whisk everything together until you have a lovely smooth batter.

5 Heat the butter in large frying pan. Pour one large spoonful of batter into the pan. Cook until golden brown. Toss or use a spatula to turn over the pancake. Make more pancakes.

6 Decorate the pancakes with jam and fruit for eyes, noses and ears. Experiment by cutting up pancakes and making smaller ones for ears and wings.

strawberry nose

blueberry eyes

strawberry jam wings

banana and blueberry nose

banana ears

chocolate mouth

What do animals do all day?

What do animals do all night?

When you're asleep, all kinds of animals are out and about, hunting for food and trying to keep safe. During the day, these animals sleep and different animals come out to look for food.

Lots of moths are awake at night. Look! They like the bright light of my torch.

Can you find the wolf calling to his pack?

What noise does an owl make?

36

Make shadow animals

You will need

a bright torch, your hands and a white wall or a big white sheet.

1 In a dark room, shine the torch onto the wall or sheet.

2 Sit in front of the torch to cast shadows.

3 Experiment by making different shapes with your hands. Which animals can you make?

Animal shadow hands

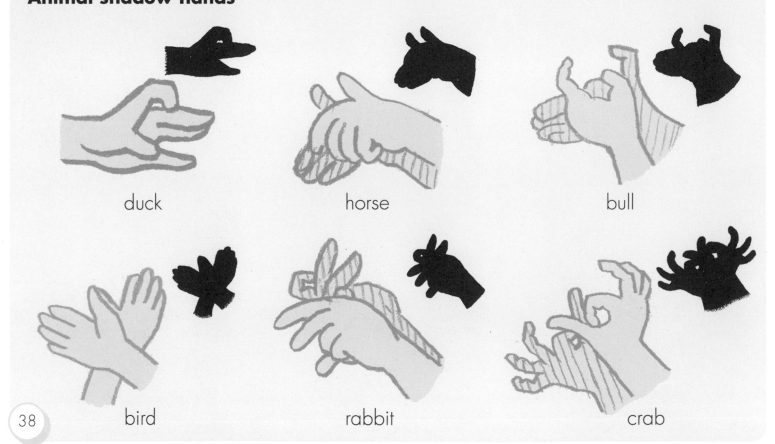

duck

horse

bull

bird

rabbit

crab

Let's have an animal sound party!

buzz

oink oink

woof woof

cock-a-doodle-doo

meow

tweet tweet

baa

moo

ribbit

How to play

Say the animal sounds below out loud in a sing-song way. Now sing the next animal sound song. Make up your own animal sound songs too.

♪ **song 1**

♪ **song 2**

♪ **song 3**

Helping each other

A fierce crocodile meets a small bird.

1 The crocodile was the fiercest animal who lived on the river.

2 'Snap, snap! Crunch, crunch!' said the fierce crocodile. The other animals kept out of his way.

3 But one day the fierce crocodile was in a really bad mood. He had terrible toothache.

4 'It hurts!', he cried.

5 When the crocodile – who, as you know, was the fiercest animal on the river – screamed, a brave little bird spotted some left-over food in his mouth.

6 'Well, hello!', said the little bird to the fierce crocodile. I've got a plan …'

7 'Open wide and don't eat me!' said the little bird. 'I can *help!*'

8 The little bird picked all the left-over food out of the crocodile's mouth.

9 The crocodile felt much better and the little bird was full. What a team!

An ants' nest

Where is the queen ant?

Ants build huge nests under the ground, where they all live together and look after the queen ant. Each ant has a job to do. Look at the picture and spot their different jobs.

42

Find these ants in the picture.

a worker ant

a soldier ant

an ant gathering food

an ant serving food

a nurse ant

Look! This ant is exploring.

How animals have babies

Different animals start life in different ways.

All animals have babies. Soon the babies grow up and have babies of their own. This is called the cycle of life. Let's find out how different baby animals are born.

A bird lays an egg.

What happens inside the egg?

A mother bird lays an egg.

chicken egg

She sits on the egg to keep it warm.

Inside, a tiny chick begins to grow.

grown-up birds

The chick is nearly ready to hatch.

The chick grows up.

The chick pecks the shell with its beak and hatches.

A frog lays eggs.

A female frog lays her eggs in water. The eggs are covered in jelly.

Tadpoles grow inside the eggs.

The tadpole grows bigger.

The tadpole swims and eats. It starts to breathe air.

The tadpole grows legs.

The tadpole grows into a froglet.

grown-up frog

Soon it will lose its tail and grow into a tiny frog.

A snake lays eggs.

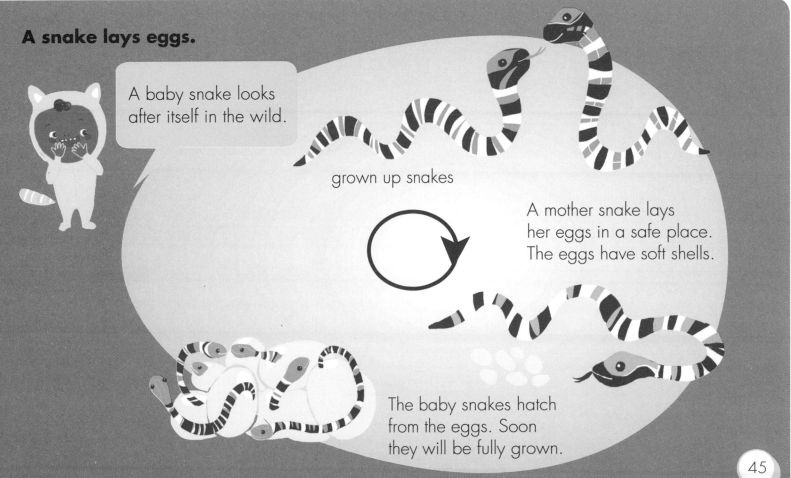

A baby snake looks after itself in the wild.

grown up snakes

A mother snake lays her eggs in a safe place. The eggs have soft shells.

The baby snakes hatch from the eggs. Soon they will be fully grown.

A mouse gives birth to baby mice.

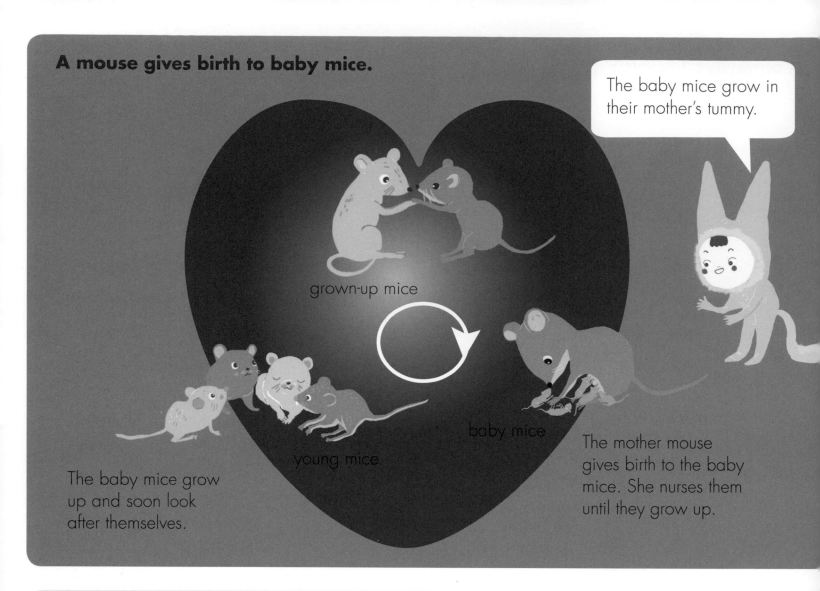

The baby mice grow in their mother's tummy.

grown-up mice

young mice

baby mice

The baby mice grow up and soon look after themselves.

The mother mouse gives birth to the baby mice. She nurses them until they grow up.

A fish lays eggs.

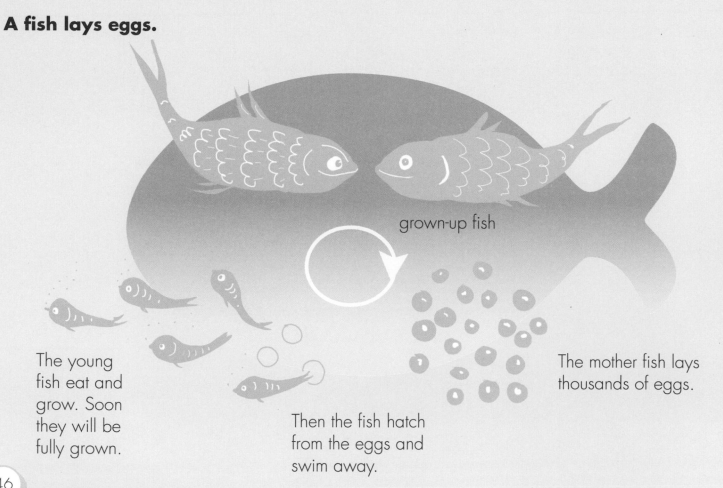

grown-up fish

The young fish eat and grow. Soon they will be fully grown.

Then the fish hatch from the eggs and swim away.

The mother fish lays thousands of eggs.

A butterfly's life cycle

Look at the pictures to see the story of a butterfly.

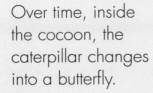

A female butterfly lays her eggs on a leaf.

The eggs hatch and become wriggling caterpillars.

The butterfly emerges from the cocoon.

A caterpillar eats and eats.

Over time, inside the cocoon, the caterpillar changes into a butterfly.

Once the caterpillar has eaten enough, it builds a small house called a cocoon.

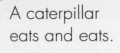

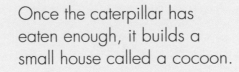

47

Animal families

Who's looking after the babies?

Different animals look after their babies in different ways but they all try to keep them safe.

Baby chick

Soon after a chick hatches from its egg, it can walk. The chick follows its mother around.

Piglet

A mother pig gives birth to ten or so piglets. Each one drinks milk from its mother.

Baby wolf

A baby wolf is called a cub. All the adults in a wolf family, called a pack, look after the cub.

Baby elephant

A baby elephant is called a calf. The calf hangs onto its mother's tail to stay safe. It takes a long time for a calf to grow up into an adult.

When a kitten plays, it is learning the skills it will need when it is grown up.

Baby koala

A baby koala is called a joey. It grows up inside a pouch on its mother's tummy.

Baby penguin

A mother and father penguin take it in turns to look after their baby penguin.

Baby seahorse

The father seahorse carries the eggs in a pouch until they hatch into baby seahorses.

I can hear a baby crocodile calling for its mother before it hatches from its egg.

Baby crocodile

The baby crocodile stays safe in the water by sitting on its mother.

Why are animals special?

Did you know animals can become invisible?

Animals have clever ways to keep safe and to creep up on animals they want to eat. Some can blend into their surroundings so that other animals don't spot them. This is called camouflage.

Who lives where?

Who lives in each place?

in the sea

desert

rainforest

polar lands

Where would each animal hide?

Match up each animal with the place where it lives.

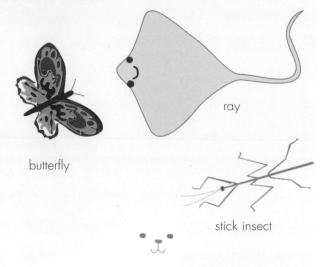

ray

butterfly

stick insect

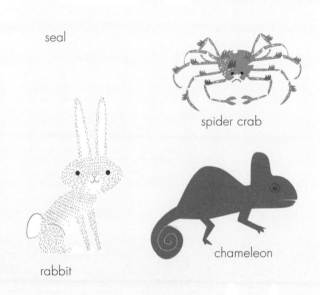

seal

spider crab

rabbit

chameleon

starfish

Arctic fox

snake

Make animal-pebbles!

You will need

- a friend
- poster paints and brushes
- 4 clean pebbles

1   Paint the pebbles to look like small animals.

2   Take it in turns with your friend to hide the pebbles in a garden or park.

Look at how these animal-pebbles blend into their surroundings. Hide your pebbles in a place where they will be camouflaged, too.

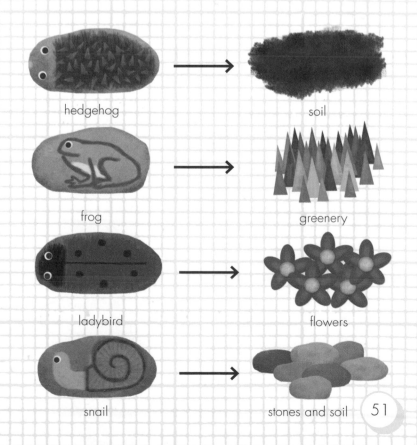

hedgehog → soil

frog → greenery

ladybird → flowers

snail → stones and soil

51

Who's hiding where?

The African plains look golden brown. Many animals that live here have golden or brown fur or skin to blend in with the dry, dusty grass.

Find these animals hiding on the African plains.

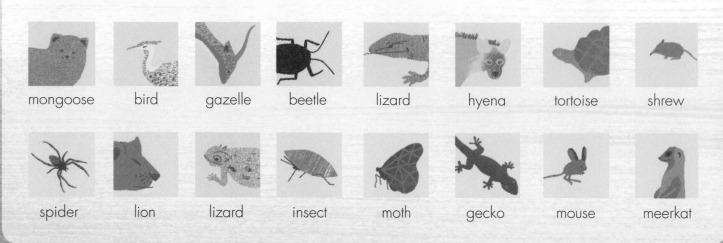

mongoose   bird   gazelle   beetle   lizard   hyena   tortoise   shrew

spider   lion   lizard   insect   moth   gecko   mouse   meerkat

Animal senses

What are the five senses?

You touch with your skin, see with your eyes, smell with your nose, taste with your tongue and hear with your ears. Many animals have super senses.

The five senses

- touch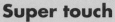
- **sight**
- hearing
- smell
- taste

Super touch

A cat uses its whiskers to see if it can fit through a tight space.

Super sight

An owl has huge eyes in its small body. An owl can see a tiny mouse, far away on a football pitch, even when it's dark.

54

Super hearing

An elephant hears low rumbling sounds that we can't. When an elephant stomps, an elephant nearby can hear the ground rumble through its legs and trunk.

Super smelling

Imagine a shark as a huge nose swimming in the ocean! A shark can smell the tiniest drop of blood from far away.

Super tasting

A fly can taste with its feet! If the fly tastes something it likes with its feet, it slurps it up with its tongue.

55

The mini-beast circus

Roll up, roll up to see the most amazing insects and spiders of all time.

Insects and spiders do all kinds of fantastic tricks. Here are some of the fastest, strongest, most acrobatic mini-beasts in the world.

I can make a parachute out of my web. Whee!

Look at those spiders go! Watch their eight legs scuttle!

fly

spider

If you could jump as high as me, you'd jump to the top of a skyscraper.

flea

spider

We are the roly polies, we roll ourselves up into a ball and roll!

My eyes are made from hundreds of mini-eyes. I can see what's happening behind me.

fly

roly polies

Dinosaurs, long long ago

When did dinosaurs live on Earth?

Millions of years ago, dinosaurs lived on Earth. We know about these huge beasts because we've found remains of their bones preserved in the ground. These bones are called fossils.

Dinosaur mystery

What kind of dinosaur made this footprint?

Whose big bones are these?

Dinosaur fossils tell us all kinds of things about how dinosaurs lived.

Some dinosaurs were gentle and ate only plants.

Which creature could come from such a big egg?

A baby dinosaur hatched from an egg.

Dinosaurs couldn't fly, but their reptile relatives, the pterosaurs (*tair-oh-saws*) could fly.

Which dinosaur could have such a big tooth?

A dinosaur that ate other dinosaurs had sharp teeth.

Some dinosaurs were fierce. They hunted and ate other dinosaurs.

No one knows why dinosaurs died out, but scientists have lots of ideas.

What if the animals left?

Koko daydreamed. What if the animals got tired of living on Planet Earth?

1  **2**

One day the animals were so fed up with people not looking after Planet Earth, they left in a big rocket.

3 No birds sang in the trees …

4 No fish swam in the sea …

5 There were no bees, which meant no flowers …

6 Soon everywhere and everything was dirty, grey and sad.

7 Everyone was sad. Everyone felt grey.

8 The explorers told everyone that if they cleaned up Planet Earth, the animals might come back.

9 So the people set to work …

10 They planted trees, kept things tidy and took care of the planet.

11 Soon Planet Earth was green again.

12 It just so happened that the animals were passing. They saw that Planet Earth was green and returned home.

13 Everyone was so pleased. The people looked after the planet and the animals lived happily ever after.

Answers

Animal families
pages 10–11

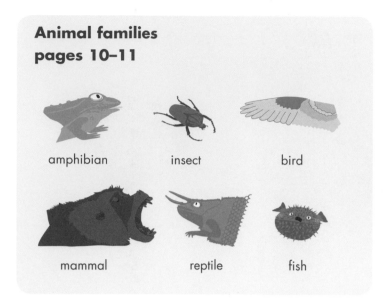

amphibian   insect   bird

mammal   reptile   fish

Animal detective
pages 16–17

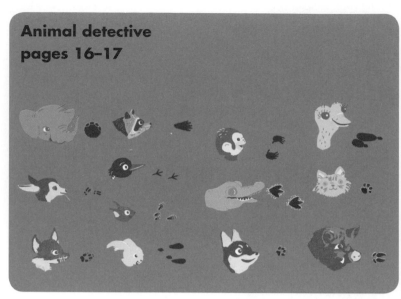

Amazon rainforest
pages 24–25

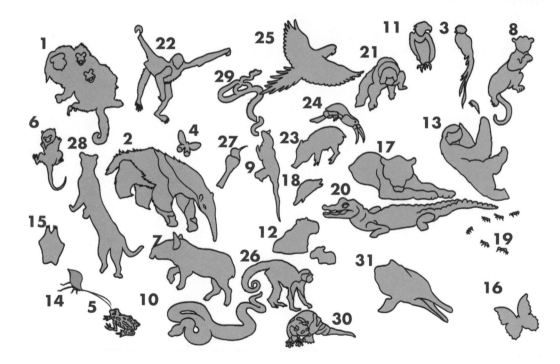

Busy ocean
pages 26–27

The red octopus has eight legs.

What is happening on the sandy seabed? Seaweed is growing, crabs are crawling, fish are hiding and starfish and shellfish are living.

There are four crabs.

10   12   3

1   3

What do animals do all day?
pages 36–37

twit twoo!

Did you get them all right?

Who lives in each place?
pages 50–51

ray
starfish
spider crab

butterfly
chameleon
stick insect

rabbit
snake

seal
Arctic fox

Ants' nest
pages 42–43

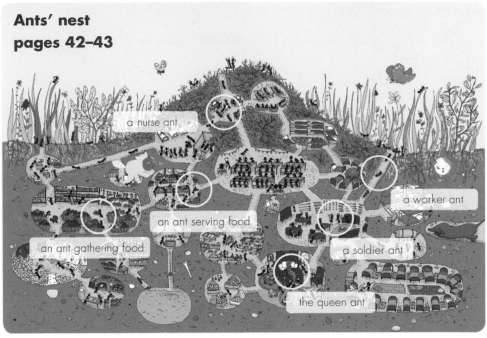

a nurse ant

an ant serving food

an ant gathering food

a worker ant

a soldier ant

the queen ant

Who's hiding where?
pages 52–53

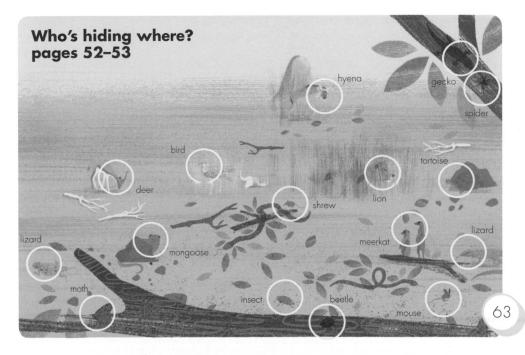

hyena

gecko

spider

bird

tortoise

deer

lion

shrew

lizard

meerkat

lizard

mongoose

moth

insect

beetle

mouse

Index

Look up a word to find out about the topic. Go through the alphabet to find the word you want.

First published in the United Kingdom in 2014 by
Thames & Hudson Ltd, 181A High Holborn, London WC1V 7QX

First paperback edition 2017

My animal book © 2014 OKIDO
the arts and science magazine for kids
www.okido.co.uk

British Library Cataloguing-in-Publication Data
A catalogue record for this book is available from the British Library
ISBN 978-0-500-65131-5

Printed and bound in China by Imago

To find out about all our publications, please visit www.thamesandhudson.com. There you can subscribe to our e-newsletter, browse or download our current catalogue, and buy any titles that are in print.

Written by Dr Sophie Dauvois
Illustration and Design by OKIDO Studio: Alex Barrow, Sophie Dauvois, Maggie Li and Rachel Ortas
Consultant: Barbara Taylor

Cover design by Rebecca Anne Louise Watson
Additional illustrations:
What is an animal? Make a paper animal, What do animals eat?, What do animals do all day? Make shadow animals, Who lives in each place?, Animal senses, Animals long ago and all the Kokos by Alex Barrow
Where do animals live, How do animals survive, Amazon rainforest, Who's hiding where?, Play mealtime stories by Maggie Li
Play animal detective! Helping each other, How do animals have babies? Animal babies, The mini-beast circus, What if the animal left? and all the explorers by Rachel Ortas
Busy ocean and Underground ants by Mathilde Nivet
Home, sweet home by Anthony Peters
Amazon rainforest animals by Sister Arrow
Make animal pancakes, Let's have an animal sound party, Make animal-pebles by Eve Isaak
Make an animal flip book by Amy Manning
Animal families and Play the animal group game by Rebecca Anne Louise Watson